D0459525

0

# THE PICTURE STORY OF FRANK ROBINSON

**Books by Bernice Elizabeth Young**

*THE PICTURE STORY OF FRANK ROBINSON*

*THE PICTURE STORY OF HANK AARON*

*HARLEM: The Story of a Changing Community*

# THE PICTURE STORY OF FRANK ROBINSON

## by B.E.Young

**Illustrated with photographs**

*JULIAN MESSNER*
*NEW YORK*

*Published by Julian Messner, a Division of Simon & Schuster, Inc.
1 West 39 Street, New York, N.Y. 10018. All rights reserved.*

*Photo Credits*
United Press International Photos: pp. 15, 38, 47, 59, 61
Wide World Photos: pp. 16, 20, 23, 25, 26, 29, 33, 35, 39, 41, 42, 43, 45, 46, 49, 50, 51, 52, 53, 54, 55, 56, 57, 58
Photos on page 12 From MY LIFE IS BASEBALL by Frank Robinson with Al Silverman. Copyright © 1968 by Frank Robinson and Al Silverman. Reproduced by permission of Doubleday & Company, Inc.

Printed in the United States of America

**Library of Congress Cataloging in Publication Data**

Young, Bernice Elizabeth.
  The picture story of Frank Robinson.

  SUMMARY: A brief biography of the baseball star who in 1974 became major league baseball's first black manager.

  1. Robinson, Frank, 1935-    —Juvenile literature. 2. Baseball—Juvenile literature.
[1. Robinson, Frank, 1935-    2. Baseball—Biography] I. Title.
GV865.R59Y68        796.357'092'4 [B] [92]        75-2236
ISBN 0-671-32736-4 lib. bdg.
ISBN 0-671-32737-2 pbk.

*To The Rev. John Andrew: "...sent to bear witness of that Light..."*

3

27 years after Jackie Robinson (right) joined the Brooklyn Dodgers and became baseball's first black player, Frank Robinson (above) was named by the Cleveland Indians to be the major leagues' first black manager.

On Thursday, October 3, 1974, Frank Robinson was named manager by the Cleveland Indians—major league baseball's first black manager. Twenty-seven years before, another Robinson, Jackie Robinson, had become the game's first black player. The men were not related, but they were both superstars and pioneers of the baseball world. "If I had one wish in the world today," Frank Robinson said, "that wish would be to have Jackie Robinson here to see this happen."

When his appointment to the managerial slot was announced, Robinson said, "I don't think I was hired because I was black. I hope not. I think I've been hired because of my ability."

Frank Robinson, Jr. was born in Beaumont, Texas, on August 31, 1935. He was the only child of Ruth Shaw and Frank Robinson, but his mother had nine older children by two previous marriages. Only two of his half brothers, Johnny and Sylvester, were living at home when Frank was born. The other four boys and three half sisters were already married and raising their own families.

The Robinson family lived in Silsbee, Texas, 20 miles north of Beaumont. Silsbee was a "railroad town"—a hot, gray place where the sun was usually hidden by the thick smoke from train engines. Most of the people who lived there either worked for the railroad or provided services for those who did. Mr. Robinson was part owner of both a funeral parlor and a grocery store. He also owned several houses which he rented to other people.

But, Mr. Robinson began to spend less and less time with his family. Finally he left them. Mrs. Robinson had to find odd jobs in order to support herself and the children.

Hard as it was, Mrs. Robinson always managed a little extra for the children—and especially for the baby, Frank. When he was only a year old, she bought him a toy baseball bat and mitt. At once, the bat became his favorite toy. As soon as he could stand up, he began to hit stones with it. By the time he was three, he was playing stick ball in the streets of Silsbee. Sometmes Frank and his friends were lucky and found an old tennis ball to play with. Otherwise, they made their own ball of rags tied together with string.

In 1939, Mrs. Robinson moved her famly to Alameda, California, where she hoped to earn more money. After two years in Alameda, the Robinsons moved again, to nearby West Oakland. Mrs. Robinson rented an apartment at 1515 Myrtle Street. It was there that Frank grew up.

Myrtle Street was like most of the other streets in Oakland at the time. It was made up of rows of crowded two-story tenement houses facing each other across a narrow street. Blacks, Mexican-Americans and Asians lived together on Myrtle Street, and there were never any racial problems. But there was trouble. It came from pool halls, card tables and crap games which could be found in every part of the city. Watching other young boys get into trouble because of them, Frank decided that he would rather spend his time playing baseball. And when he wasn't playing baseball, he kept to himself.

Frank was his mother's favorite and she almost always let him have his own way—and his way was baseball. As he grew older, he spent more and more time in the Tompkins Street School playground or in the streets, playing ball. He never took a job to help support the family as his two half brothers did. His mother never insisted that he do so. "Sometimes I told her I had a ball game, and I did it just to get out of cutting the lawn. But she never said anything."

It was during these early days that Frank developed his attitude towards baseball. As he put it, "Right from the first, I'd play all-out. I'd slide in on asphalt and never think about it. If I raised a strawberry on my backside, I'd just go home and bandage it and—here we go again! Once, I tore the whole side of my pants sliding, and when my mother saw me, she nearly had a fit!"

When Frank was 14, George Powles, the baseball and basketball coach of McClymonds High School in West Oakland, invited him to try out for a sandlot baseball team. The team was sponsored by the Doll Drug Company, and they played in Bushrod Park in North Oakland on Sunday mornings. Frank was still in junior high school, but he was already earning a reputation as a fine hitter.

The day Frank arrived at the park for his try-out, Mr. Powles gave him a uniform. But he did not put him in the starting line-up. Instead, he told the boy to sit on the bench. Disappointed and restless, Frank watched the game for the first four innings. Then, in the fifth, Powles sent him in as a pinch hitter. Frank connected with the first pitch and smashed it over the center fielder's head for a home run. Mr. Powles decided to leave him in the game. His other at-bat was a line drive triple against the left field fence. After the game, Mr. Powles told Frank that he had made the team.

At fourteen, Frank was 6'1" tall and very, very thin. Mr. Powles gave him a set of exercises to build up his arms and shoulders. When Frank wasn't playing baseball, he did pushups or squeezed a rubber ball to strengthen his hands.

In September, 1950, Frank entered McClymonds High School. He made the baseball team in his sophomore year and the basketball team when he was a junior. He also went out for football, but on his first tackle, he dislocated his shoulder. On another play, he got stepped on and gouged between the eyes by a cleat. He decided that football was not for him.

*Frank played basketball as well as baseball for McClymonds High School. During the 1950-51 season, his team won the City championship. Coach George Powles is at top left next to Frank.*

*Frank played third base while he was in high school. He is second from left in this photo of the McClymonds infield.*

Throughout his high school career, Frank's main interest was baseball. He played third base because, as he says, "You couldn't play the outfield in high school. That wasn't the glamorous position. So I played third base."

Mr. Powles worked with him, teaching him the basics of fielding and base running. But, he never had to work on Frank's hitting. The boy was a natural power hitter. He just stood at the plate and swung.

On the day Frank graduated from high school, he received an offer to join the St. Louis Browns. But, Mr. Powles advised him not to accept it, since the Browns' organization was very large and a young player might get lost in it. This was followed by offers from two other clubs: the Chicago White Sox and the Cincinnati Reds. Each club was willing to pay him a bonus of $3,500 to sign with them. However, the White Sox wanted him to play with their Class D team, while Cincinnati offered him a slot on their Class C team. Since Frank felt that he had played better than Class D ball in high school, he accepted the Cincinnati offer. His starting salary was $400 a month.

Frank's first assignment was to Ogden, Utah, in the Pioneer League. He joined the Ogden team in the middle of the 1953 season. Although he was only 17, he was put directly into the line-up. On his first time at bat, he blasted a fast ball for a triple, 412 feet off the center field wall. The next day, he lifted one over the left field fence for a home run —his first as a professional player.

Frank started out with Ogden at third base. But, unlike during his high school days, he couldn't get used to playing that position against professional teams. He was so discouraged that he asked Manager Earle Brucker to switch him to the outfield. Although Brucker had been very happy with Frank's play at third, he agreed to move him to left field.

Playing left, Frank had to learn how to judge fly balls. Sometimes he played too deep, and the ball fell in front of him. More often, in his eagerness to catch a deep fly, he crashed into the wall. But, he felt that any ball hit in the park should be caught, and he disregarded the possibility of injury. He recalls, "Some players will do anything to win, and that's just the way I played the game." After a while, he felt happy and comfortable in his new position.

Off the field, Robinson was much less comfortable and not at all happy. There weren't many

*It took Frank a while to get used to playing the outfield. Sometimes fly balls fell short of him and, at other times, they were just over his head.*

blacks living in Ogden. Those who were there were discriminated against. This was a new experience for Frank Robinson.

One evening, Frank, who enjoyed the movies, went up to the window of Ogden's only movie theater to buy a ticket. The cashier turned him away saying, "We don't cater to Negroes here." Frank was deeply hurt.

He spent most of his time learning more and more about baseball—how to carry out a squeeze play or a hit-and-run, how to slide, and how to hit a breaking ball. He says, "I always thought I knew how to slide, but I didn't. Once I twisted my knee sliding into second base, and I rammed it a few other times. But by the end of the season, I had learned."

*Frank's skill at sliding was well-learned. When a game is tight, the way a runner slides into a base can make all the difference—especially when he is trying to score.*

By the end of the season, the Ogden team was the champion of the Pioneer League. Frank's batting average was a strong .348, and he led the team in home runs with 17 and in RBIs with 83.

For the 1954 season, Frank was assigned to Tulsa. This was a big step forward, since Tulsa was a Double A Class team. They needed a strong hitter in their line-up, but they wanted him to play second base. Frank lasted for 8 games with Tulsa. He was all thumbs at second base, and it affected his hitting. He went into a batting slump. The Cincinnati management decided to send him to their Columbia, South Carolina team in the Sally League.

When Robinson arrived there, he was one of four black players, the first the team had ever had. In Columbia, the fans were pleasant because they respected the men's playing ability. But on the road, the four blacks were constantly insulted. They couldn't go into restaurants. Instead, they had to stay in the team's bus, waiting for their white teammates to bring them sandwiches. They were not allowed to stay in hotels but had to room in private homes or at the YMCA. They had to find black cab drivers to take them to the ball park, since they weren't allowed to ride in cabs driven by whites. And Frank Robinson hated it! But, he made up his mind to accept it for a year. He was determined that he would be moving to the majors and out of the South by the end of the 1954 season.

He played so well that year that his batting average was .336, and he had 110 RBIs. He led the Sally League with 112 runs scored. As a result, he was scheduled to start the 1955 season with the Redlegs in Cincinnati.

In the meantime, Robinson went to Puerto Rico to play the winter season there. On one raw, chilly day he was trying to get a runner at the plate. From deep left, he cut loose the throw. Something snapped in his right shoulder and he was unable to move his arm. By the next day, the arm had swollen to twice its size, and it was extremely painful. The doctor who examined him could not find what was wrong with the arm. He told Frank that the best thing would be to rest it.

When Robinson reported to the Reds' spring training camp, he still could not use his arm properly. He saw a number of doctors, but none of them could find what was wrong. Frank was in no condition to play major league ball. So, the Reds sent him back to Columbia.

Frank was so discouraged at this setback that he was ready to leave the team and go home. After all his hard work to get out of the South, he was going back to racial insults and eating sandwiches in the bus. It seemed to be more than he could take, and he almost gave up baseball.

But he finally decided not to quit—he was too close to realizing his ambition of being a major league player. For two weeks, he gave his arm a complete rest. Then he began working out, a little at a time. To his delight, the arm began to respond. Later in the season, he was able to fire off a throw from deep left to cut off a runner who was trying to score. That day, he knew that whatever had been wrong with his arm had healed.

In February, 1956, Robinson reported to spring training in Tampa, Florida, to start his first season as one of the Cincinnati Reds.

That season, for the first time, Robinson would be facing major league pitching. Although he had always been a power hitter, he did not feel he was sharp enough to deliver against the men he would be facing. "Pitchers like to have the whole plate to work with—to come in on you and then go away from you. I decided I wouldn't give them the complete plate to shoot at. I felt that if I gave them the inside of the plate—at least until I got two strikes

*Bearing in over the plate, Robinson combines strong wrist action and a full follow-through for power hitting.*

on me—and protected the outside corner, I would be better off."

Robinson began standing closer in, about even with home plate, with his feet close to the chalk line. Bending forward slightly from the waist, he held the bat back on his shoulder. His head was in what is known as "concussion alley"—almost directly over the plate. In this position he would be constantly in danger of being hit by pitched balls, but he played the game to win, no matter what it took. He worked on his new stance through spring training. His hitting, always good, became even better.

On April 12, Reds' General Manager Gabe Paul told Robinson that he was being added to the team roster. Five days later, on the traditional Monday opening day in Cincinnati, he was in the starting line-up against the St. Louis Cardinals, batting seventh.

Frank came up in the bottom half of the second, right after teammate Ray Jablonski had hit a home run. The fans were still cheering for Jablonski when Robinson dug in. Vinegar Bend Mizell, pitching for the Cards, may have been upset by the home run. Certainly he wasn't worried about facing a rookie. He served up a fast ball right down the middle, and Frank bounced it off the center field wall for a double. In his next two trips to the plate, Frank singled and drew a base on balls.

During that first season Robinson had a lot to learn about running the bases and stealing. In a game against the Philadelphia Phillies, the Reds were behind, 3 to 2, in the eighth inning. Robinson was on second, Ed Bailey at the plate. Frank took a long lead off second. Watching the Phillies' pitcher carefully, he decided that he could make it to third safely. He broke for it, but was thrown out. After the game, Manager Birdie Tebbetts told him, "Any time you're on second base and you try to steal third, you shouldn't be thrown out."

Robinson was also having his problems fielding. Six times he crashed into the wall and was stunned or knocked out completely. But he always recovered and went on playing. Finally Tebbetts told him, "Look, Frank, the next time you hit a wall, I'm not going to leave the dugout. I'm getting too old to walk 450 feet for nothing."

Frank ended his first season with the Reds with a batting average of .290. He had hit 38 home runs, had 83 RBIs, scored 122 runs and was the unanimous choice for the National League Rookie of

*Robinson feels that every ball hit in the park should be caught—even when he has to go into the stands to get it!*

*In his first year as a major league player, Frank Robinson equalled the record for home runs by a rookie when he hit his 38th on September 11th. The record had been set by Wally Berger who played with the Boston Braves in 1930. On hand to congratulate Robinson is teammate Ted Kluzewski. Giants' catcher is Bill Sarni and Bill Jackowski is the umpire.*

the Year. Sports writers were beginning to compare his hitting with that of Ted Williams and Stan Musial.

Robinson's second year disproved the theory of the "sophomore jinx"—that all good rookies slump the second, or sophomore, year. In fact, he was voted National League Sophomore of the Year. Although he had only 29 homers, his batting average was up to .322. He had 75 RBIs and scored 97 runs.

After the 1957 season, Robinson was eligible to be drafted into the armed services. Rather than wait for the draft, he joined the Marines. One day, on the obstacle course, he discovered that he had no strength in his right arm. He said nothing. But during a medical examination, a doctor found out about his old shoulder injury. X-Rays were taken, and they showed calcium deposits around the shoulder joint. The doctor told Frank that his career as a baseball player could come to an end at any time because of the shoulder. Two weeks later, Robinson was out of the Marines on an honorable discharge for medical reasons. And he went back to playing baseball.

*Going home—Frank's old shoulder injury cut short his stay in the Marines.*

On April 9, 1958, the Reds played an exhibition game against the Washington Senators in Portsmouth, Ohio. Camilo Pascual was on the mound for the Senators as Robinson came up to bat in the first inning. Frank dug in the batter's box in his usual stance. Pascual threw a hard, fast ball. With a loud crack, it hit Robinson under his protective helmet, just below the ear. The players stood frozen in terror, as he slumped, unconscious, to the ground. As teammate and best friend, Vada Pinson, put it later, "I tried to walk out and see him, but my legs wouldn't take me. I thought he was dead." Frank was carried off the field on a stretcher and taken to a hospital.

*Robinson is attended by Redlegs' trainer Wayne Andersen on the way to the hospital after being hit by Camilo Pascual's pitch.*

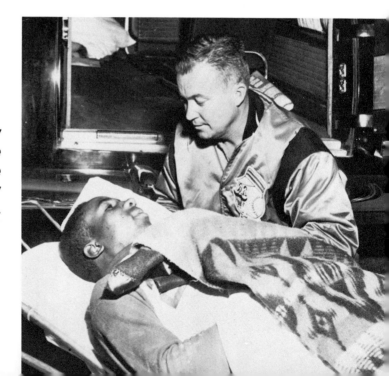

Although Robinson was out of the hospital in three days, the season was almost over before he was fully recovered. After being hit so hard, he went through a period during which he was afraid to crowd the plate. But, after a while, he overcame the fear and had his head right back in "concussion alley." And he managed to hit 23 home runs in the latter part of the season. He ended the year batting .269.

1958 was a bad year for the Reds, too. They finished near the bottom of the league. As so often happens with a losing team, the following year, they got a new manager, Fred Hutchinson. They also gave up their first baseman in a trade, and Hutchinson assigned Robinson to first. Frank didn't want to make the move, but he had no choice. That season, he made 17 errors. Joking about it later, he said, "On the first-to-second-to-first double play, I was beautiful. I would take the ball and make the pivot to throw—and the ball would end up behind me and all over—everywhere but second base." The main problem was that Robinson did not *want* to play first. "I just wasn't the kind of player that could make the transition from outfield to infield easily," he remembers.

Fortunately, his lack of enthusiasm for his new position did not show up in his hitting. In one game against the Dodgers, he hit the cycle—single, double, triple and round tripper. Later in the season, he blasted St. Louis Cardinals' pitching for three consecutive home runs. In August, he swatted his first major league grand slam. For the season, he batted a respectable .311 with 36 home runs and 125 RBIs.

Robinson's problems continued with the 1960 season. He was still playing first base and hating it. In the first half of the season, he was plagued with injuries. He was still having shoulder problems; he pulled a leg muscle; and he hurt a heel, a thumb and an ankle. He did not get along as well with Fred Hutchinson as he had with the previous manager, Birdie Tebbetts. And, to make matters worse for him, Bill DeWitt took over from Gabe Paul as General Manager of the Reds.

From the moment they met, Robinson and DeWitt did not hit it off. DeWitt was a very formal person who did not encourage friendship with his players. And when the time came for the two men to discuss a new contract for 1961, DeWitt insisted that Robinson should take a cut in salary. Among other things, he accused Robinson of not "hus-

*The grip that helped hit the cycle—and was to make Robinson's hitting feared throughout the league.*

*Another injury for Robinson. The same ankle had been injured a few weeks earlier.*

tling." That comment infuriated Frank, who always goes all-out when he is on the field. He finally signed a contract for the same amount of money he had been making in 1960, but he was very upset.

Then, Robinson was arrested. Since he usually carried large sums of money with him, he had bought a small gun for protection. However, he failed to get a permit to carry it, and in the state of Ohio this was against the law.

On February 9, Frank and two friends went to a basketball game in Cincinnati. After the game they stopped at a diner where an argument broke out between one of Robinson's friends and some of the other customers. The friend was arrested. Frank and his other friend bailed him out of jail, and they returned to the diner to finish their meal.

While they were eating, Robinson looked up to see the cook staring at him. The man made a threatening motion, dragging his index finger across his throat. He began to move toward Frank, a butcher's knife in one hand.

Robinson pulled his gun and the cook screamed for help. The police were called again. When they saw Frank's gun, they arrested him.

A friendly sports writer found out about the arrest and placed a call to the Red's General Manager. DeWitt resented having his sleep interrupted and refused to do anything about it. Frank spent the night in a detention cell.

He says, ". . . the most disturbing thought of all, the one that haunted me all night long, was what would the kids think of me? So many kids idolize big-league ball players. So many of them mold their whole lives around their heroes. What were they going to think?"

The next morning, DeWitt arranged for bail for Frank, and he was let out of jail. Three weeks later, he appeared before a grand jury, charged with illegal possession of the gun. He pleaded guilty and paid a fine. On the way out of the courthouse, he promised himself that 1961 would be his best season yet, to make it up to his fans.

That year, sports writers were describing the Reds as "ragamuffins" and predicting that they would finish in sixth place. But, the Cincinnati team opened the season by taking five out of seven games. They dropped the next eight straight, then snapped back to take nine in a row.

Robinson was hot, batting close to .300 in mid-May. The Reds were looking more and more like a championship team. By mid-June, they moved into first place. Between June 15 and the All-Star break, they took 21 out of 28 games. They were leading the league by five games.

That July, Robinson chalked up an average of .409. He had 13 homers and batted in 31 runs. And the rest of the team was playing the same kind of heads-up baseball. The Reds were on their way to a pennant, and they knew it. They unanimously chose Frank Robinson to be their team captain.

After the All-Star break, the Reds went into a losing streak. For a while, the Dodgers took the lead away from them.

Robinson began holding informal meetings with the players—no managers or coaches present. They discussed faults and problems. If a man was in a slump, the other players suggested what he might try to pull out of it. If a player was having difficulty fielding against particular hitters, his teammates advised him on how to play them. The meetings helped to clear the air and relax the men so they could play a better game.

And it showed on the field. Cincinnati began to win the games they had to in order to stay alive in the pennant race. Frank Robinson was leading the way.

On August 8, he was out of the line-up because of a bad ankle, but he was sent in to pinch-

*Frank began a long-standing practice of holding informal meetings with the players. They were not always serious. Here he sets himself up as a judge, mop for a wig and bat for a gavel, passing sentence — probably a $1 fine to go into the "pot" for a post-season party. The pleading defendant is second baseman Dave Johnson.*

hit. His single led to the tying run. Two days later, again as a pinch-hitter, his double drove in the tying run. He later scored the winning run in a 5 to 3 squeaker against the Giants. On August 12, he broke up a game against the Dodgers by singling in the eighth inning, stealing second, and then scoring the winning run.

By September 26, the Reds were three games ahead of the Dodgers. On that day, they faced the Chicago Cubs while the Dodgers met the Pittsburgh Pirates. The Reds were trailing, 3 to 2, when Robinson came to bat in the seventh with one man on. Frank worked the count to 3 and 2 before he drilled a fast ball over the center field wall for a two-run homer. In the next inning, teammate Jerry Lynch hit another two-run home run. That night, the Dodgers dropped their game to Pittsburgh. The pennant was Cincinnati's!

The Reds went on to meet the New York Yankees in the World Series. But they were no match for the Yankees. The Reds won only one game.

The year 1961 brought another thrill to Frank Robinson, greater even than winning the pennant. Early in November, he was told that he had won the National League's Most Valuable Player Award.

*In 1962, the Most Valuable Player
Award went to Frank Robinson for
the National League and Roger Maris
for the American League.*

He had won against Orlando Cepeda and Vada Pinson.

During the winter break, Frank married Barbara Ann Cole of Los Angeles. He had met her there earlier in the year, when the Reds played the Dodgers. Shortly after they were married, they decided to adopt a child. Frank, a family man now, was worried about his future. He was feeling the effects of the many injuries he had suffered. And he was having a problem with DeWitt over his 1962 contract. As usual, he and DeWitt were wide apart on how much money his services were worth. All this made Frank begin to think seriously about retiring from baseball. However, he finally signed his contract with a raise of $12,500.

The Reds got off to a slow start in the 1962 season. Their start was slow enough to allow the Dodgers to gain a healthy edge over them. The Dodgers usually won the big ones from the Redlegs. But Frank played well against them.

One game in late August went into extra innings. After the first two Reds had reached base safely, Dodgers' manager, Walt Alston, instructed pitcher Larry Sherry to give Vada Pinson an intentional base on balls, to set up the double-play. With bases loaded, Robinson stepped up to the plate. Trying to drive in the winning run, Robinson went for the first two pitches for a count of two strikes. The next two pitches were sliders that broke outside. That evened the count to 2 and 2. Then Sherry delivered another slider. This one broke in over the plate. It connected with Robinson's bat and cleared the stadium scoreboard—383 feet away and 55 feet high.

Frank ended 1962 with a .342 batting average. He had 39 home runs and 136 RBIs, scored 134 runs and stole 18 bases. Nevertheless, he was still planning to retire. Few ball players took him seriously. And Gene Mauch, Manager of the Philadelphia Phillies, commented, "I know 91 pitchers in the league and 9 managers who will chip in $500 apiece if Robinson will go through with his plans to retire. That's $50,000!"

During the seventh inning of what was supposed to be Frank's last game, he came up to bat to the sound of the organist playing "Auld Lang Syne." Throughout the stadium, players and fans stood at attention. Stepping out of the batter's box, Frank threw back his head and laughed. After the game, he casually mentioned to manager Fred Hutchinson that he would be reporting for spring training in 1963.

As the 1963 season progressed, Robinson may have been sorry that he had not retired, for his health continued to jinx him. There was that old trouble with his shoulder, plus a swollen elbow. Then, he was hit on the fist by an inside pitch and suffered a jammed thumb. Later, he pulled a muscle in his leg which did not clear up for several weeks. Finally, on September 7, he slid into second base and collided with the Mets' Ron Hunt. As Robinson hit the ground, Hunt accidentally stepped on

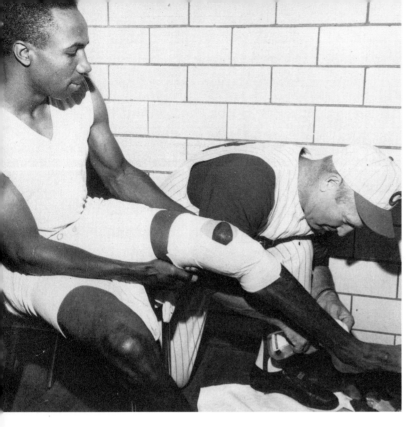

*Robinson played hard and to win, and he was constantly plagued with injuries. Most times, he simply had the wound bandaged and went back into the game.*

his arm. The cleats tore Frank's arm open and it took 30 stitches to close the wound.

Robinson's troubles showed up in his batting average. His .259 that year was the lowest he had ever had. When Bill DeWitt offered Frank less money for 1964, he had the figures to back up his arguments.

The Cincinnati management was also a little unhappy with Robinson, whom they considered a "troublemaker." Frank spoke out when he thought something was wrong, but he was the team captain and was acting as its spokesman. He was trying to solve problems, not cause them.

Frank went into the 1964 season determined that it would be a good year for him. He hit .306 with 29 home runs and 96 RBIs. When he negotiated for his 1965 contract, Frank asked that his entire cut be restored. DeWitt refused. There was a long and bitter argument. The bargaining ended with Frank's getting about half of his pay cut restored. He did not sign the contract until about a week before spring training began.

*Although Frank did not get the salary he wanted, he finally signed a new contract for the 1965 season, after he, Assistant General Manager Phil Seghi (left) and President Bill DeWitt (right) reached an agreement.*

Feelings remained bitter between Robinson and the Reds' management throughout the 1965 season. The Reds missed winning another pennant by one game. And Robinson's average dropped down to .296, although he slammed 33 home runs and chalked up 113 RBIs.

On December 9, Frank was having dinner with his wife Barbara, their son Frank Kevin and baby daughter Nichelle, when the phone rang. It was Phil Seghi, Assistant General Manager of the Reds. "Frank," he said, "you've been traded to Baltimore." He went on to talk about the wonderful job Robinson had done for the club over the years. Then he hung up.

Frank was both hurt and surprised. Although he knew that his outspoken ways had angered some people, he had no idea that the Reds would trade him because of it. And the trade was out of the National League into the American League.

When Robinson reported to the Baltimore Orioles for spring training, Manager Hank Bauer greeted him by asking him about his arm. Nothing could have made Frank feel better than this concern. He went on to have a very good spring training, hitting better than he ever had at that time of the year.

*Manager Hank Bauer welcomed Robinson to the Orioles.*

Frank enjoyed playing for Hank Bauer. "You could discuss your problems with Hank," he said, "and he was very tolerant of mistakes. He wouldn't get too mad when you made a mistake because he knew you were a professional and no matter how young you were, you wouldn't be likely to make that mistake again."

With Frank Robinson batting third and Brooks Robinson in the clean-up slot, the Orioles went ahead of the league early in the 1966 season. They were in and out of first place in April and May, and settled at the top about the middle of June.

It was on May 8, in a game in Baltimore, that Frank Robinson hit the first fair ball ever hit out of Memorial Stadium—a tape-measure homer, 540 feet from home plate. When the announcement was made over the public address system, 49,000 fans surged to their feet to give the Baltimore slugger a thunderous ovation. It made Frank feel at home. That day, he went 5 for 7, to raise his batting aver-

*After setting a record for the longest home run ever hit in Baltimore's Memorial Stadium, Frank Robinson jumped on home plate with both feet. Luis Aparicio congratulates him.*

*He caught it! Frank comes up on the spectators' side of the right-field wall after a spectacular, game-saving catch against the Yankees on June 21, 1966.*

age to over .400 and take the lead in the American League batting race.

That season, Robinson played his first All-Star game in an American League uniform, although he had played it six times for the National League while he was with Cincinnati. But it was "The other Robinson [who] made all the noise." Brooks Robinson had three hits in the game, while Frank went 0 for 4.

The Orioles were leading the league by eight games at the All-Star break. By the first of August, they had pulled ahead by 13½. They were headed for a pennant.

On September 21, the Orioles played the Kansas City Athletics. The A's took an early lead and were ahead 6 to 1 at the bottom of the sixth. But, in the top of the seventh, Frank Robinson hit a two-run homer. He got another during a seven-run rally in the eighth inning. The next day, he connected for two doubles and a single, driving in two runs. That brought his total home runs for the season to 49 and his total RBIs to 122. His batting average was .316.

With the most home runs, most runs batted in, and the highest batting average in the American League, Robinson won the Triple Crown, the eleventh major leaguer to do so. And by sweeping the three-game series from Kansas City, Baltimore clinched the American League pennant. Their opponents in the World Series would be the Los Angeles Dodgers, against whom Frank had played many times.

Facing Dodgers' pitcher Don Drysdale in the opener, Robinson went for the first pitch. He connected with it, and drove the ball 340 feet into the stands for his 50th homer of the year. He says of that hit, "I don't think I reached first base when I saw it fall in. I think I floated around the bases. I

*Big guns in the first game of the World Series: Frank Robinson, who hit his 50th home run of the season during the game, and Moe Drabowsky, whose one-hit relief pitching protected the 5 to 2 victory.*

don't remember a thing until I got back to the dugout!"

In the fourth game of the Series, with the Orioles ahead 3 games to 0, Drysdale was back on the mound for the Dodgers. The game was scoreless into the bottom of the fourth. Russ Snyder led off the Orioles' half of the inning by popping out. Then Robinson stepped into the batter's box. He knocked the dirt out of his cleats, then stepped up to the plate, crowding it, his head in "concussion alley." With the bases clear, Drysdale could take a full windup. He threw a fast ball right over the middle of the plate, belt high. Frank stepped into it and lifted it right out of the park. Sparked by Robinson's bat, the Orioles took the series in four straight. And Robinson was chosen to receive the

*Dave McNally and Frank Robinson made it four straight for the Orioles.*

*Frank has just been presented with the Babe Ruth Award for being the outstanding World Series player in 1966.*

Babe Ruth award of the New York chapter of the Baseball Writers' Association of America as the outstanding player of the Series.

*The Houston Chapter of the Baseball Writers' Association named Robinson "Player of the Year" for 1966. Awards were also presented to Dizzy Dean (left) — the "Tris Speaker Award," Gaylord Perry (right center) — "Pitcher of the Year;" and Lou Torres (right) — the "Eddie Dyer Award."*

The Orioles started the 1967 season slowly. Then, on June 28, in a game against the Chicago White Sox, Robinson tried to stretch a single into a double. Going into second full force, he rammed into Al Weis. Both men had to be carried out of the game—Weis with torn ligaments of the knee and Robinson with a concussion.

While Frank was out of the line-up, the Orioles lost 17 out of 28 games. Later during the season, Robinson was quoted in a newspaper as saying that the Orioles weren't playing up to their full potential that year. Many people became angry with him because of what he said. But the fact was that the Orioles were never serious contenders for the pennant that year.

The Orioles' slump continued into the beginning of the 1968 season. At the All-Star break, Earl Weaver was named to replace Hank Bauer as manager. Weaver had spent two winter seasons (October to January) managing in the Puerto Rican League, but now that he was the Orioles' manager, he could no longer handle it. He spoke with Frank Robinson about taking over the job.

Frank was eager to try his hand at managing. He was thinking of his future. He had had two poor seasons in a row, his injuries bothered him, he was thirty-three years old and in the 13th season of major league play. And, too, he felt that the day would soon come when a black would be made manager of a major league team, and he wanted a chance at it. When Hiram Cuevas, owner of the Santurce team, the Crabbers, offered him the manager's job on Weaver's recommendation, Frank took it.

He expected problems because he was black, but he had none. As he said, his abilities, not his

*Sealing the agreement to manage the Santurce club, Frank Robinson shakes hands with Hiram Cuevas, owner. At left is Earl Weaver, and in the rear is Harry Dalton, Director of Player Personnel for the Orioles.*

color, were the only important thing in baseball. His players respected him for his skill in handling them, his leadership, and his knowledge of the game.

Robinson showed great know-how, but he learned, too. He learned not to argue too much with umpires, not to ask too much of his players, and not to leave his pitchers in too long—among other things. He led Santurce to a pennant in his first year as manager, and he continued to manage them for six more seasons.

*Santurce manager Robinson and umpire Ron Hansen exchange words. This is one of the times Robinson felt strongly enough to argue a point—and Hansen felt strongly enough to throw him out!*

But his role as a big league player was far from over. In 1969, he led his teammates once again to the American League championship, although not to a World Series victory. On June 26, 1970, against Washington, he hit back-to-back grand slam homers.

And 1971, his sixteenth year in the major leagues, was one of his greatest years. On September 13, in a Monday night double-header against the Detroit Tigers, he smashed the 499th and 500th home runs of his career. He was only the 11th player to reach that mark, following Babe Ruth, Jimmy Foxx, Mel Ott, Ted Williams, Willie Mays, Mickey Mantle, Hank Aaron, Eddie Mathews, Ernie Banks, and Harmon Killebrew.

*The Baltimore Orioles romped over the Minnesota Twins by a score of 11 to 2 to take the American League Championship in 1969. Among the happiest men on the team were Manager Earl Weaver and Frank Robinson.*

*On September 13, 1971, Robinson became the 11th player in major league history to belt 500 home runs, and the first to reach 499 and 500 in the two games of a double header. Here he is shown hitting Number 499 in the first game.*

*Number 500 in the second game.*
*Teammate Boog Powell was at home*
*plate to congratulate him.*

Frank's 28 homers in 1971, along with 99 RBIs and a .281 batting average, helped to take the Orioles into their third straight World Series—which they lost to Pittsburgh. At the end of the season he was voted the Most Valuable Player of the American League, the first player in the history of the game to receive that award from both leagues.

*Frank Robinson is the only baseball player to win the Most Valuable Player Award in both the American and National Leagues.*

*Japanese slugger Sadaharu Oh of the Yomiuri Giants greeted Boog Powell, Baseball Commissioner Bowie Kuhn, and the Orioles' two Robinsons, Frank and Brooks, during an exhibition season in Tokyo in October, 1971—just before Frank was traded to the Dodgers.*

Despite that honor, Robinson was traded to the Los Angeles Dodgers. He was soon to be 37, and the Orioles wanted to find room for several players from their farm system. So, on December 2, 1971, Frank found himself back in the National League. He said that he was happy with the trade to his hometown because "There's nothing wrong with going from a winner to a winner."

*Robinson, his wife, Barbara, and their children, Nichelle and Kevin, read about the trade that took Frank back to the National League—this time with the Los Angeles Dodgers.*

Frank continued to play for the Dodgers and to play well. But, in 1973, the Dodgers traded him to the California Angels. He spent only one season there, but in that short time, he was elected team captain.

*The same old Robinson! On his first appearance as a Dodger, he lashed out a single which scored a run.*

*Mid-way through his season with the California Angels, Robinson was elected by his teammates to be their team captain. Manager Dick Williams made the announcement.*

*In May, 1973, J. Frank Cashen, Vice President of the Baltimore Orioles, removed No. 20 from his team's roster of numbers. Robinson, an Angel outfielder at the time of the ceremony, had been No. 20 for six years with the Orioles.*

Robinson was traded once more—to the Cleveland Indians in September, 1974. Sports writers began to speculate about whether or not he was to be more than the "designated hitter" he was hired to be, whether in fact he would become manager. The Cleveland management had long been unhappy with Manager Ken Aspromonte. But Frank donned the Indians' uniform as a designated hitter.

Then, on October 3, the announcement came that Frank Robinson would be the new manager of the Cleveland team. When he was asked how he felt about being the first black man to hold such a position. Robinson's reaction was that he did not want to be known only as the major league's first black manager, that his color should have nothing to do with his ability to do the job. "If I don't do well, the fans will know and the management can fire me."

Frank Robinson has often observed, "My life is baseball." He has already made history in it. And the future holds promise of more.

*Robinson's selection as manager of the Cleveland Indians was announced by Phil Seghi (who had been Assistant General Manager of Cincinnati when Frank played with the Redlegs). Seghi said, "He has technical knowledge, yes, but above all, he has the leadership quality I was looking for."*

## FRANK ROBINSON
### Born August 31, 1935, at Beaumont, Tex.
### Height, 6.01. Weight, 194.
### Throws and bats righthanded.

## BATTING RECORD

| Year | Club | League | Pos. | G | AB | R | H | 2B | 3B | HR | RBI | B.A. |
|------|------|--------|------|---|----|----|---|----|----|----|-----|------|
| 1953 | Ogden | Pion. | O-3B-1B | 72 | 270 | 70 | 94 | 20 | 6 | 17 | 83 | .348 |
| 1954 | Tulsa | Tex. | 2B-3B | 8 | 30 | 4 | 8 | 0 | 0 | 0 | 1 | .267 |
| 1954 | Columbia | Sally | OF-3-2B | 132 | 491 | *112 | 165 | 32 | 9 | 25 | 110 | .336 |
| 1955 | Columbia | Sally | OF-1B | 80 | 243 | 50 | 64 | 15 | 7 | 12 | 52 | .263 |
| 1956 | Cincinnati | Nat. | OF | 152 | 572 | *122 | 166 | 27 | 6 | 38 | 83 | .290 |
| 1957 | Cincinnati | Nat. | OF-1B | 150 | 611 | 97 | 197 | 29 | 5 | 29 | 75 | .322 |
| 1958 | Cincinnati | Nat. | OF-3B | 148 | 554 | 90 | 149 | 25 | 6 | 31 | 83 | .269 |
| 1959 | Cincinnati | Nat. | 1B-OF | 146 | 540 | 106 | 168 | 31 | 4 | 36 | 125 | .311 |
| 1960 | Cincinnati | Nat. | 1-OF-3 | 139 | 464 | 86 | 138 | 33 | 6 | 31 | 83 | .297 |
| 1961 | Cincinnati | Nat. | OF-3B | 153 | 545 | 117 | 176 | 32 | 7 | 37 | 124 | .323 |
| 1962 | Cincinnati | Nat. | OF | 162 | 609 | *134 | 208 | *51 | 2 | 39 | 136 | .342 |
| 1963 | Cincinnati | Nat. | OF-1B | 140 | 482 | 79 | 125 | 19 | 3 | 21 | 91 | .259 |
| 1964 | Cincinnati | Nat. | OF | 156 | 568 | 103 | 174 | 38 | 6 | 29 | 96 | .306 |
| 1965 | Cincinnati† | Nat. | OF | 156 | 582 | 109 | 172 | 33 | 5 | 33 | 113 | .296 |
| 1966 | Baltimore | Am. | OF-1B | 155 | 576 | *122 | 182 | 34 | 2 | *49 | *122 | *.316 |
| 1967 | Baltimore | Am. | OF-1B | 129 | 479 | 83 | 149 | 23 | 7 | 30 | 94 | .311 |
| 1968 | Baltimore | Am. | OF-1B | 130 | 421 | 69 | 113 | 27 | 1 | 15 | 52 | .268 |
| 1969 | Baltimore | Am. | OF-1B | 148 | 539 | 111 | 166 | 19 | 5 | 32 | 100 | .308 |
| 1970 | Baltimore | Am. | OF-1B | 132 | 471 | 88 | 144 | 24 | 1 | 25 | 78 | .306 |
| 1971 | Baltimore‡ | Am. | OF-1B | 133 | 455 | 82 | 128 | 16 | 2 | 28 | 99 | .281 |
| 1972 | Los Angeles§ | Nat. | OF | 103 | 342 | 41 | 86 | 6 | 1 | 19 | 59 | .251 |
| 1973 | California | Amer. | OF | 147 | 534 | 85 | 142 | 29 | 0 | 30 | 97 | .266 |
| 1974 | California● | Amer. | OF | 144 | 477 | 81 | 117 | 27 | 3 | 22 | 68 | .245 |
| Major League Totals | | | ........ | 2723 | 9821 | 1805 | 2900 | 523 | 72 | 574 | 1778 | .295 |

†Traded to Baltimore Orioles for Outfielder Dick Simpson and Pitchers Milt Pappas and Jack Baldschun. December 9, 1965.

‡Traded with Pitcher Pete Richert to Los Angeles Dodgers for Pitchers Doyle Alexander and Bob O'Brien, Catcher Sergio Robles and First Baseman-Outfielder Royle Stillman. December 2, 1971.

§Traded with Infielders Billy Grabarkewitz and Bob Valentine and Pitchers Bill Singer and Mike Strahler to California Angels for Third Baseman Ken McMullen and Pitcher Andy Messersmith, November 28, 1972.

● Purchased by Cleveland Indians on waivers from the California Angels. September 12, 1974.

## CHAMPIONSHIP SERIES RECORD

| Year | Club | League | Pos. | G | AB. | R. | H. | 2B. | 3B. | HR. | RBI. | B.A. | PO. | A. | E. | F.A. |
|------|------|--------|------|---|-----|----|----|-----|-----|-----|------|------|-----|----|----|------|
| 1969 | Baltimore | Amer. | OF | 3 | 12 | 1 | 4 | 2 | 0 | 1 | 2 | .333 | 2 | 0 | 1 | .667 |
| 1970 | Baltimore | Amer. | OF | 3 | 10 | 3 | 2 | 0 | 0 | 1 | 2 | .200 | 2 | 0 | 0 | 1.000 |
| 1971 | Baltimore | Amer. | OF | 3 | 12 | 2 | 1 | 1 | 0 | 0 | 1 | .083 | 7 | 0 | 0 | 1.000 |
| Championship Series Totals | | | | 9 | 34 | 6 | 7 | 3 | 0 | 2 | 5 | .206 | 11 | 0 | 1 | .917 |

## WORLD SERIES RECORD

Tied World Series record for most times hit by pitcher, game (2), October 8, 1961.
Hit home run in first World Series at bat, October 5, 1966.

| Year | Club | League | Pos. | G | AB. | R. | H. | 2B. | 3B. | HR. | RBI. | B.A. | PO. | A. | E. | F.A. |
|------|------|--------|------|---|-----|----|----|-----|-----|-----|------|------|-----|----|----|------|
| 1961 | Cincinnati | Nat. | OF | 5 | 15 | 3 | 3 | 2 | 0 | 1 | 4 | .200 | 5 | 0 | 0 | 1.000 |
| 1966 | Baltimore | Amer. | OF | 4 | 14 | 4 | 4 | 0 | 1 | 2 | 3 | .286 | 6 | 0 | 0 | 1.000 |
| 1969 | Baltimore | Amer. | OF | 5 | 16 | 2 | 3 | 0 | 0 | 1 | 1 | .188 | 13 | 0 | 0 | 1.000 |
| 1970 | Baltimore | Amer. | OF | 5 | 22 | 5 | 6 | 0 | 0 | 2 | 4 | .273 | 7 | 0 | 0 | 1.000 |
| 1971 | Baltimore | Amer. | OF | 7 | 25 | 5 | 7 | 0 | 0 | 2 | 2 | .280 | 12 | 0 | 0 | 1.000 |
| World Series Totals | | | | 26 | 92 | 19 | 23 | 2 | 1 | 8 | 14 | .250 | 43 | 0 | 0 | 1.000 |

## ALL-STAR GAME RECORD

| Year | League | Pos. | AB. | R. | H. | 2B. | 3B. | HR. | RBI. | B.A. | PO. | A. | E. | F.A. |
|------|--------|------|-----|----|----|-----|-----|-----|------|------|-----|----|----|------|
| 1956 | National | OF | 2 | 0 | 0 | 0 | 0 | 0 | 0 | .000 | 1 | 0 | 0 | 1.000 |
| 1957 | National | OF | 2 | 0 | 1 | 0 | 0 | 0 | 0 | .500 | 5 | 0 | 0 | 1.000 |
| 1959 | National (2nd game) | 1B | 3 | 1 | 3 | 0 | 0 | 1 | 1 | 1.000 | 3 | 0 | 1 | .750 |
| 1961 | National (1st game) | OF | 1 | 0 | 1 | 0 | 0 | 0 | 0 | 1.000 | 2 | 0 | 0 | 1.000 |
| 1962 | National (2nd game) | OF | 3 | 0 | 0 | 0 | 0 | 0 | 0 | .000 | 1 | 0 | 0 | 1.000 |
| 1965 | National | PH | 1 | 0 | 0 | 0 | 0 | 0 | 0 | .000 | 0 | 0 | 0 | .000 |
| 1966 | American | OF | 4 | 0 | 0 | 0 | 0 | 0 | 0 | .000 | 2 | 0 | 0 | 1.000 |
| 1969 | American | OF | 2 | 0 | 0 | 0 | 0 | 0 | 0 | .000 | 0 | 0 | 0 | .000 |
| 1970 | American | OF | 3 | 0 | 0 | 0 | 0 | 0 | 0 | .000 | 1 | 0 | 0 | 1.000 |
| 1971 | American | OF | 2 | 1 | 1 | 0 | 0 | 1 | 2 | .500 | 2 | 0 | 0 | 1.000 |
| 1974 | American | OF | 1 | 0 | 0 | 0 | 0 | 0 | 0 | .000 | 0 | 0 | 0 | .000 |
| All-Star Totals | | | 24 | 2 | 6 | 0 | 0 | 2 | 3 | .250 | 17 | 0 | 1 | .969 |

Member of National League All-Star Team in 1959 (first game) and 1961 (second game); did not play. Named to American League Team for 1967 game; replaced due to injury.